Fun Stuff
Frozen Pops

Publications International, Ltd.

Copyright © 2012 Publications International, Ltd.
All rights reserved. This publication may not be reproduced or quoted in whole or in part by any means whatsoever without written permission from:

Louis Weber, CEO
Publications International, Ltd.
7373 North Cicero Avenue
Lincolnwood, IL 60712

Permission is never granted for commercial purposes.

Recipe development on pages 28, 30, 40, 50, 56, 64, 70, 72, 80, 84, 86, 92, 120, 112 and 124 by Bev Bennett.

Recipe development on pages 6, 12, 20, 22, 24, 26, 30, 32, 34, 36, 38, 42, 44, 46, 48, 52, 54, 58, 60, 62, 68, 74, 76, 78, 82, 88, 90, 94, 96, 98, 100, 102, 104, 106, 108, 110, 112, 116 and 118 by Allison S. Kahen RD, LDN.

Recipe development on pages 4, 8, 14 and 18 by Jamie Schleser.

All photographs *except* those on pages 17 and 115 by PIL Photo Studio, Chicago
Photographer: Justin Paris
Photographer's Assistants: Lauren Kessler, Annemarie Zelasko
Food Stylists: Kathy Joy, Mary Ann Melone, Walter Moeller, Josephine Orba, Carol Smoler
Assistant Food Stylists: Sheila Grannen, Lissa Levy, Breana Moeller
Prop Stylist: Paula Walters

Pictured on the front cover *(clockwise from top left):* Salted Caramel Pops *(page 50),* Wild Watermelon Pops *(page 6),* St. Patty's Pops *(page 110)* and Fruit-Filled Pops *(page 26).*
Pictured on the jacket flaps: Carrot Cake Pops *(page 98)* and Chocolate-Covered Pretzel Pops *(page 46).*
Pictured on the back cover *(left to right):* Blackberry Layered Pops *(page 22),* Citrus Mango Pops *(page 14)* and S'more Pops *(page 52).*

ISBN-13: 978-1-4508-3861-0
ISBN-10: 1-4508-3861-8

Library of Congress Control Number: 2011942588

Manufactured in China.

8 7 6 5 4 3 2 1

Microwave Cooking: Microwave ovens vary in wattage. Use the cooking times as guidelines and check for doneness before adding more time.

Publications International, Ltd.

Contents

Fruit Fest

Paradise Pops

  1 cup milk
¾ cup frozen or fresh pineapple chunks
¾ cup frozen or fresh chopped mango
¼ cup unsweetened coconut milk
  1 tablespoon honey
    Pop molds or paper or plastic cups
    Pop sticks

1. Combine milk, pineapple, mango, coconut milk and honey in blender or food processor; blend until smooth.

2. Pour mixture into molds. Cover top of each mold with small piece of foil. Freeze 1 hour.*

3. Insert sticks through center of foil. Freeze 6 hours or until firm.

4. To remove pops from molds, remove foil and place bottoms of pops under warm running water until loosened. Press firmly on bottoms to release. (Do not twist or pull sticks.)

Makes 4 pops

If using pop molds with lids, skip step 3 and freeze until firm.

Paradise Pops

Wild Watermelon Pops

2 cups diced seedless watermelon (1-inch cubes)
2 tablespoons strawberry fruit spread
1 cup vanilla frozen yogurt
4 (5-ounce) paper or plastic cups or pop molds
4 teaspoons mini semisweet chocolate chips
4 pop sticks

1. Combine 1 cup watermelon and fruit spread in blender or food processor; blend until smooth. Add remaining 1 cup watermelon; blend until smooth and well combined. Add frozen yogurt, ½ cup at a time, blending until smooth after each addition.

2. Pour mixture into cups. Freeze 1 hour or until mixture just begins to harden.

3. Stir mixture in cups until smooth and slushy. Stir 1 teaspoon chocolate chips into each cup. Smooth top of mixture with back of spoon. Cover top of each cup with small piece of foil. Freeze 1 hour.

4. Insert sticks through center of foil. Freeze 4 hours or until firm.

5. To serve, remove foil and peel away paper cups or gently twist frozen pops out of plastic cups.

Makes 4 pops

 *Tip* To use cone-shaped paper cups, line a baking sheet with regular-shaped 5-ounce paper cups, bottom sides up. Cut a small hole in the bottom of each regular-shaped paper cup. Place a cone-shaped cup, tip side down, in the hole to hold the pop in place.

·Fruit Fest·

Wild Watermelon Pops

Lemon Strawberry Pops

1 cup frozen strawberries
1 cup milk
½ cup plain yogurt
1 tablespoon sugar
1 tablespoon lemon juice
4 (5-ounce) paper or plastic cups or pop molds
4 pop sticks

1. Combine strawberries, milk, yogurt, sugar and lemon juice in blender or food processor; blend until smooth.

2. Pour mixture into cups. Cover top of each cup with small piece of foil. Freeze 2 hours.

3. Insert sticks through center of foil. Freeze 6 hours or until firm.

4. To serve, remove foil and peel away paper cups or gently twist frozen pops out of plastic cups.

Makes 4 pops

Lemon Strawberry Pops

Fruit Freezies

   1 can (15 ounces) apricot halves in light syrup, rinsed and drained
¾ cup apricot nectar
   3 tablespoons sugar, divided
     Ice cube trays
   1 can (15 ounces) sliced pears in light syrup, rinsed and drained
¾ cup pear nectar
1½ cups frozen chopped mango
¾ cup mango nectar
     Picks or mini pop sticks

1. Combine apricots, apricot nectar and 1 tablespoon sugar in blender or food processor; blend until smooth. Evenly pour mixture into one third of ice cube trays.

2. Combine pears, pear nectar and 1 tablespoon sugar in blender or food processor; blend until smooth. Evenly pour mixture into one third of ice cube trays.

3. Combine mango, mango nectar and remaining 1 tablespoon sugar in blender or food processor; blend until smooth. Evenly pour mixture into remaining one third of ice cube trays.

4. Freeze 1 to 2 hours or until almost firm.

5. Insert picks. Freeze 1 to 2 hours or until firm.

6. To remove pops from trays, place bottoms of ice cube trays under warm running water until loosened. Press firmly on bottoms to release. (Do not twist or pull picks.)

Makes 12 servings

Variation: Try any of these favorite fruit combinations or create your own! Use crushed pineapple and pineapple juice or add more flavor to the combinations above. Add coconut extract to the apricot mixture or almond extract to the pear mixture.

Fruit Freezies

Double Berry Pops

2 cups plain nonfat Greek yogurt, divided
1 cup blueberries
3 tablespoons sugar, divided
6 (5-ounce) paper or plastic cups or pop molds
1 cup sliced strawberries
6 pop sticks

1. Combine 1 cup yogurt, blueberries and 1½ tablespoons sugar in blender or food processor; blend until smooth.

2. Pour mixture into cups. Freeze 2 hours.

3. Combine strawberries, remaining 1 cup yogurt and 1½ tablespoons sugar in blender or food processor; blend until smooth.

4. Pour mixture into cups over blueberry layer. Cover top of each cup with small piece of foil. Freeze 2 hours.

5. Insert sticks through center of foil. Freeze 4 hours or until firm.

6. To serve, remove foil and peel away paper cups or gently twist frozen pops out of plastic cups.

Makes 6 pops

Double Berry Pops

Citrus Mango Pops

1½ cups mango nectar
¾ cup frozen chopped mango
½ cup lemon sorbet
3 tablespoons lime juice
1 tablespoon honey
¼ teaspoon grated lime peel
   Pop molds or paper or plastic cups
   Pop sticks

1. Combine mango nectar, mango, sorbet, lime juice, honey and lime peel in blender or food processor; blend until smooth.

2. Pour mixture into molds. Cover top of each mold with small piece of foil. Freeze 2 hours.*

3. Insert sticks through center of foil. Freeze 6 hours or until firm.

4. To remove pops from molds, remove foil and place bottoms of pops under warm running water until loosened. Press firmly on bottoms to release. (Do not twist or pull sticks.)

Makes 4 pops

If using pop molds with lids, skip step 3 and freeze until firm.

Citrus Mango Pops

Magic Rainbow Pops

1 envelope (¼ ounce) unflavored gelatin
¼ cup cold water
½ cup boiling water
1 container (6 ounces) raspberry or strawberry yogurt
1 container (6 ounces) lemon or orange yogurt
1 can (8¼ ounces) apricots or peaches with juice
Pop molds with lids

1. Combine gelatin and cold water in 2-cup glass measuring cup. Let stand 5 minutes to soften. Add boiling water. Stir until gelatin is completely dissolved. Cool.

2. For first layer, combine raspberry yogurt and ¼ cup gelatin mixture in small bowl; stir until completely blended. Fill each pop mold about one third full with raspberry mixture.* Freeze 30 to 60 minutes or until set.

3. For second layer, combine lemon yogurt and ¼ cup gelatin mixture in small bowl; stir until completely blended. Pour lemon mixture over raspberry layer in each mold.* Freeze 30 to 60 minutes or until set.

4. For third layer, combine apricots with juice and remaining ¼ cup gelatin mixture in blender or food processor; blend until smooth. Pour mixture over lemon layer in each mold.* Cover with lids. Freeze 2 to 5 hours or until firm.**

5. To remove pops from molds, place bottoms of pops under warm running water until loosened. Press firmly on bottoms to release. (Do not twist or pull lids.)

Makes about 6 pops

*Pour any extra mixture into small paper cups. Freeze as directed in the Tip.
**If you aren't using pop molds with lids, cover each pop with small piece of foil and insert sticks through center of foil.

Tip: Three-ounce paper or plastic cups can be used in place of the molds. Make the layers as directed or put a single flavor in each cup and cover each cup with small piece of foil and freeze 1 hour before inserting sticks. Freeze until firm. To serve, remove foil and peel away paper cups or gently twist frozen pops out of plastic cups.

•Fruit Fest•

Magic Rainbow Pops

Purplicious Pops

  1 cup frozen blueberries
  ¾ cup pomegranate juice
  ½ cup raspberry sherbet
  ½ cup milk
  2 tablespoons honey
     Pop molds or paper or plastic cups
     Pop sticks

1. Combine blueberries, pomegranate juice, sherbet, milk and honey in blender or food processor; blend until smooth.

2. Pour mixture into molds. Cover top of each mold with small piece of foil. Freeze 2 hours.*

3. Insert sticks through center of foil. Freeze 6 hours or until firm.

4. To remove pops from molds, remove foil and place bottoms of pops under warm running water until loosened. Press firmly on bottoms to release. (Do not twist or pull sticks.)

Makes 4 pops

If using pop molds with lids, skip step 3 and freeze until firm.

Purplicious Pops

Tropic Pops

2 bananas, cut into chunks
1½ cups unsweetened coconut milk
1½ cups pineapple juice
2 tablespoons sugar
½ teaspoon vanilla
⅛ teaspoon ground nutmeg
¼ cup shredded sweetened coconut
8 (5-ounce) plastic or paper cups or pop molds
8 pop sticks

1. Combine bananas, coconut milk, pineapple juice, sugar, vanilla and nutmeg in blender or food processor; blend until smooth. Stir in shredded coconut.

2. Pour mixture into cups. Cover top of each cup with small piece of foil. Freeze 2 hours.

3. Insert sticks through center of foil. Freeze 6 hours or until firm.

4. To serve, remove foil and gently twist frozen pops out of plastic cups or peel away paper cups.   *Makes 8 pops*

 **Tip** Make these plain pops more appealing by using plastic cups, which give the pops a ridged texture.

Tropic Pops

Blackberry Layered Pops

1¼ cups plain nonfat Greek yogurt, divided
¼ cup milk
2 tablespoons sugar, divided
6 teaspoons lime juice, divided
1 cup chopped blackberries, divided
Pop molds or paper or plastic cups
Pop sticks

1. Combine ¾ cup yogurt, milk, 1 tablespoon sugar and 3 teaspoons lime juice in blender or food processor; blend until smooth. Gently stir in ¼ cup blackberries.

2. Pour mixture into molds. Freeze 1 hour.

3. Combine ½ cup blackberries and 1½ teaspoons lime juice in blender or food processor; blend until smooth.

4. Pour mixture into molds over yogurt layer. Freeze 1 hour.

5. Combine remaining ½ cup yogurt, ¼ cup blackberries, 1 tablespoon sugar and 1½ teaspoons lime juice in blender or food processor; blend until smooth.

6. Pour mixture into molds over blackberry layer. Cover top of each mold with small piece of foil. Insert sticks through center of foil. Freeze 4 hours or until firm.

7. To remove pops from molds, remove foil and place bottoms of pops under warm running water until loosened. Press firmly on bottoms to release. (Do not twist or pull sticks.)

Makes 4 pops

Blackberry Layered Pops

Apricot Pops

1 can (about 8 ounces) apricot halves in heavy syrup
1 cup apricot nectar
½ cup plain nonfat Greek yogurt, divided
    Pop molds or paper or plastic cups
    Pop sticks

1. Drain apricots; discard syrup. Rinse apricots under cool running water; chop and set aside.

2. Combine apricot nectar, yogurt and ¼ cup chopped apricots in blender or food processor; blend until smooth. Stir in remaining chopped apricots.

3. Pour mixture into molds. Cover top of each mold with small piece of foil. Freeze 1 hour.*

4. Insert sticks through center of foil. Freeze 4 hours or until firm.

5. To remove pops from molds, remove foil and place bottoms of pops under warm running water until loosened. Press firmly on bottoms to release. (Do not twist or pull sticks.)

Makes 4 pops

If using pop molds with lids, skip step 4 and freeze until firm.

•Fruit Fest•

Apricot Pops

Fruit-Filled Pops

¼ cup blueberries
2 strawberries, thinly sliced
4 kiwi slices
Pop molds
⅔ cup light-colored juice or flavored beverage
Pop sticks

1. Evenly arrange blueberries, strawberries and kiwi in molds.*

2. Pour juice evenly into molds. Cover top of each mold with small piece of foil. Insert sticks through center of foil. Freeze 6 to 8 hours or until firm.

3. To remove pops from molds, remove foil and place bottoms of pops under warm running water until loosened. Press firmly on bottoms to release. (Do not twist or pull sticks.)

Makes 4 pops

Plastic pop molds must be used for this recipe. The fruit will not stay in place if using paper or plastic cups.

Variation: This pretty pop works great with any combination of fruits. Choose any juice or flavored beverage that tastes best with the fruits.

Fruit-Filled Pops

Chocolate Shoppe

Tiny Toffee Pops

    1 pint (2 cups) chocolate ice cream
1½ cups chocolate-covered toffee chips
  ½ cup finely chopped blanched almonds
  ½ cup finely chopped milk chocolate
     Pop sticks

1. Line baking sheet with plastic wrap. Scoop 14 rounded tablespoonfuls ice cream onto baking sheet. Freeze 2 hours or until firm.

2. Combine toffee chips, almonds and chocolate in shallow dish; mix well. Gently roll ice cream into balls in mixture, turning to coat and pressing mixture evenly into ice cream. Return to baking sheet.*

3. Insert sticks. Freeze 2 hours or until firm.

Makes 14 pops

*If ice cream melts on baking sheet, place baking sheet and ice cream in freezer 30 minutes before continuing. If ice cream is too hard, let stand 1 to 2 minutes before rolling in mixture.

Tiny Toffee Pops

Cookies & Cream Pops

1 cup crushed mini creme-filled cookies (about 2½ cups cookies), divided
⅓ cup plus 1 tablespoon milk, divided
Pop molds or paper or plastic cups
1¼ cups vanilla ice cream
¼ cup mini semisweet chocolate chips
⅛ teaspoon ground cinnamon
Pop sticks

1. Combine ½ cup cookie crumbs and 1 tablespoon milk in small bowl, mixing and mashing with fork until blended. Press about 2 tablespoons crumb mixture into each mold, using wet fingers if necessary.

2. Combine remaining ½ cup cookie crumbs, ⅓ cup milk, ice cream, chocolate chips and cinnamon in blender or food processor; blend until smooth.

3. Pour mixture into molds over cookie base. Cover top of each mold with small piece of foil. Insert sticks through center of foil. Freeze 6 hours or until firm.

4. To remove pops from molds, remove foil and place bottoms of pops under warm running water until loosened. Press firmly on bottoms to release. (Do not twist or pull sticks.)

Makes 3 pops

Chocolate Chip Cookie Pops: Scoop 1 pint (2 cups) vanilla ice cream into chilled large metal bowl. Cut in ⅔ cup chopped hard chocolate chip cookies and ⅔ cup chopped pecans with pastry blender or two knives; fold and cut again. Repeat, working quickly, until mixture is evenly incorporated. Scoop 10 scant ¼ cupfuls ice cream mixture. Gently roll ice cream into balls in 1 cup mini semisweet chocolate chips, turning to coat and pressing chips evenly into ice cream. Place on baking sheet lined with plastic wrap. Insert sticks. Freeze 2 hours or until firm. Makes 10 pops.

·Chocolate Shoppe·

Cookies & Cream Pops

Frozen Hot Chocolate Pops

1 cup milk
2 ounces semisweet chocolate, finely chopped
3 tablespoons sugar
2 tablespoons hot chocolate mix
2 cups chocolate ice cream
  Pop molds or paper or plastic cups
  Pop sticks

1. Combine milk, chopped chocolate, sugar and hot chocolate mix in small microwavable bowl. Microwave on HIGH 30 seconds; stir. Microwave at 30-second intervals, stirring after each interval until chocolate is melted and mixture is smooth. Cool to room temperature, about 1 hour.

2. Pour chocolate mixture in blender or food processor; add ice cream. Blend until smooth.

3. Pour mixture into molds. Cover top of each mold with small piece of foil. Freeze 2 hours.*

4. Insert sticks through center of foil. Freeze 4 to 6 hours or until firm.

5. To remove pops from molds, remove foil and place bottoms of pops under warm running water until loosened. Press firmly on bottoms to release. (Do not twist or pull sticks.)

Makes 6 pops

*If using pop molds with lids, skip step 4 and freeze until firm.

•Chocolate Shoppe•

Frozen Hot Chocolate Pops

White Chocolate Macadamia Pops

¼ cup sugar
¼ cup cornstarch
½ teaspoon salt
2 cups milk
¾ cup whipping cream
6 ounces white chocolate, chopped
2 teaspoons vanilla
½ cup chopped macadamia nuts
6 (5-ounce) plastic or paper cups or pop molds
6 pop sticks

1. Combine sugar, cornstarch and salt in medium saucepan. Slowly whisk in milk and cream. Bring to a boil over medium heat, stirring constantly. Reduce heat to low; cook and stir 2 to 3 minutes or until thickened. Remove from heat.

2. Add white chocolate and vanilla, stirring constantly until chocolate is completely melted. Let stand 30 minutes to cool slightly.

3. Cover and refrigerate 2 hours.

4. Stir macadamia nuts into mixture. Pour mixture into cups. Cover top of each cup with small piece of foil. Freeze 2 hours.

5. Insert sticks through center of foil. Freeze 6 hours or until firm.

6. To serve, remove foil and gently twist frozen pops out of plastic cups or peel away paper cups.

Makes 6 pops

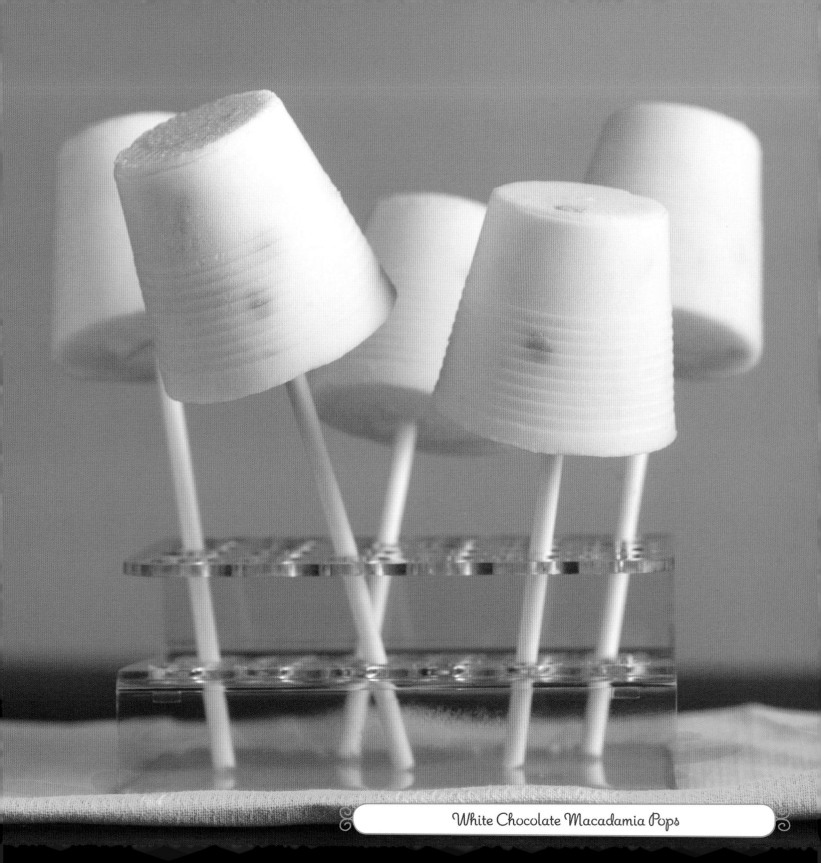

White Chocolate Macadamia Pops

Chocolate-Covered Strawberry Pops

1 cup sliced strawberries, divided
Pop molds
1 cup chocolate ice cream
¼ cup milk
3 tablespoons chocolate syrup
Pop sticks

1. Evenly arrange ½ cup strawberry slices in molds.*

2. Combine ice cream, remaining ½ cup strawberries, milk and chocolate syrup in blender or food processor; blend until smooth.

3. Pour mixture into molds. Cover top of each mold with small piece of foil. Insert sticks through center of foil. Freeze 6 to 8 hours or until firm.

4. To remove pops from molds, remove foil and place bottoms of pops under warm running water until loosened. Press firmly on bottoms to release. (Do not twist or pull sticks.)

Makes 4 pops

Plastic pop molds must be used for this recipe. The fruit will not stay in place if using paper or plastic cups.

Chocolate-Covered Strawberry Pops

Triple Chocolate Pops

1 cup chocolate ice cream
¼ cup milk
1 tablespoon chocolate syrup
½ cup crushed chocolate wafers
3 (5-ounce) plastic or paper cups or pop molds
3 pop sticks
6 tablespoons quick-hardening chocolate shell dessert topping

1. Combine ice cream, milk and chocolate syrup in blender or food processor; blend until smooth. Add crushed wafers; pulse using on/off action until just combined.

2. Pour mixture into cups, filling two-thirds full. Freeze 1 hour.

3. Insert sticks. Spoon 2 tablespoons chocolate shell topping into each cup over ice cream layer. *Do not cover with foil.* Freeze 4 to 6 hours or until firm.

4. To serve, gently twist frozen pops out of plastic cups or peel away paper cups.

Makes 3 pops

•Chocolate Shoppe•

Triple Chocolate Pops

Candy Bar Pops

1 pint (2 cups) vanilla ice cream
1 bar (about 2 ounces) chocolate-covered peanut, caramel and
    nougat candy, chopped
½ cup chopped honey-roasted peanuts
¼ cup caramel ice cream topping
    Pop sticks
3 ounces semisweet chocolate

1. Scoop ice cream into chilled large metal bowl. Cut in chopped candy, peanuts and caramel topping with pastry blender or two knives; fold and cut again. Repeat, working quickly, until mixture is evenly incorporated. Cover and freeze 1 hour.

2. Line baking sheet with plastic wrap. Scoop 10 balls ice cream mixture onto baking sheet. Freeze 1 hour.

3. Shape ice cream into balls, if necessary. Insert sticks. Freeze 1 hour or until firm.

4. Melt chocolate in top of double boiler over simmering water, stirring occasionally.

5. Drizzle melted chocolate over pops. Freeze 30 minutes to 1 hour or until firm.

Makes 10 pops

Candy Bar Pops

Choco-Razz Pops

  2 cups fresh or frozen raspberries
¾ cup milk
  1 container (6 ounces) vanilla yogurt
  3 tablespoons chocolate syrup
¼ cup mini semisweet chocolate chips
10 (3-ounce) paper or plastic cups or pop molds
10 pop sticks

1. Combine raspberries, milk, yogurt and chocolate syrup in blender or food processor; blend until smooth. Stir in chocolate chips.

2. Pour mixture into cups. Cover top of each cup with small piece of foil. Freeze 2 hours.

3. Insert sticks through center of foil. Freeze 6 hours or until firm.

4. To serve, remove foil and peel away paper cups or gently twist frozen pops out of plastic cups.

Makes 10 pops

 **Tip** This pop works great with other fruits. Try substituting frozen cherries for the raspberries and cherry yogurt for the vanilla yogurt.

·Chocolate Shoppe·

Choco-Razz Pops

Frozen Chocolate-Covered Bananas

  2 medium ripe bananas
  4 pop sticks
  ½ cup granola cereal without raisins
  1 bottle (7¼ ounces) quick-hardening chocolate shell dessert topping

1. Line baking sheet with waxed paper.

2. Peel bananas; cut each in half crosswise. Insert stick about 1½ inches into center of cut end of each banana. Place on prepared baking sheet. Freeze 2 hours or until firm.

3. Place granola in large resealable food storage bag; crush slightly using rolling pin or meat mallet. Transfer granola to shallow dish. Pour chocolate shell topping in separate shallow dish.

4. Place one frozen banana in topping; turn and spread evenly over banana with spatula. Immediately place banana in dish with granola, turning to coat evenly. Return to baking sheet. Repeat with remaining bananas.

5. Freeze 2 hours or until firm. Let stand 5 minutes before serving.   *Makes 4 servings*

 *Tip* For a fun twist on these treats, roll in sprinkles, coconut, chopped peanuts or any other desired toppings.

Frozen Chocolate-Covered Bananas

Chocolate-Covered Pretzel Pops

¼ cup plus 2 tablespoons fudge topping, divided
½ cup crushed pretzels
4 (5-ounce) paper or plastic cups or pop molds
¾ cup milk
1¼ cups chocolate ice cream
2 pretzel rods, broken in half *or* 4 pop sticks

1. Place ¼ cup fudge topping in small microwavable bowl; microwave on HIGH 15 seconds. Stir until smooth.

2. Add crushed pretzels to melted fudge topping, mixing and mashing with fork until blended. Press about 2 tablespoons mixture into each cup, using wet fingers if necessary.

3. Place remaining 2 tablespoons fudge topping in small microwavable bowl. Microwave on HIGH 15 seconds. Stir until smooth. Gradually whisk in milk.

4. Pour milk mixture in blender or food processor; add ice cream. Blend until smooth.

5. Pour mixture into cups over pretzel base. Cover top of each cup with small piece of foil. Gently insert pretzel rod half through center of foil. Freeze 6 hours or until firm.

6. To serve, remove foil and peel away paper cups or gently twist frozen pops out of plastic cups.

Makes 4 pops

Chocolate-Covered Pretzel Pops

Cool Creations

Raspberry Layered Pops

1¼ cups plain nonfat Greek yogurt, divided
¼ cup milk
2 tablespoons sugar, divided
6 teaspoons lemon juice, divided
1 cup chopped raspberries, divided
4 (5-ounce) paper or plastic cups or pop molds
4 pop sticks

1. Combine ¾ cup yogurt, milk, 1 tablespoon sugar and 3 teaspoons lemon juice in blender or food processor; blend until smooth. Gently stir in ¼ cup raspberries.

2. Pour mixture into cups. Freeze 1 hour.

3. Combine ½ cup raspberries and 1½ teaspoons lemon juice in blender or food processor; blend until smooth.

4. Pour mixture into cups over yogurt layer. Freeze 1 hour.

5. Combine remaining ½ cup yogurt, ¼ cup raspberries, 1 tablespoon sugar and 1½ teaspoons lemon juice in blender or food processor; blend until smooth.

6. Pour mixture into cups over raspberry layer. Cover top of each cup with small piece of foil. Insert sticks through center of foil. Freeze 4 hours or until firm.

7. To serve, remove foil and peel away paper cups or gently twist frozen pops out of plastic cups.

Makes 4 pops

Raspberry Layered Pops

Salted Caramel Pops

    1 pint (2 cups) vanilla ice cream
    1 cup finely chopped salted pretzels (about 2 cups whole pretzels)
¼ cup caramel ice cream topping
    Coarse salt
    Pop sticks
2 ounces semisweet chocolate

1. Scoop ice cream into chilled large metal bowl. Cut in pretzels and caramel topping with pastry blender or two knives; fold and cut again. Repeat, working quickly, until mixture is evenly incorporated. Cover and freeze 1 hour.

2. Line baking sheet with plastic wrap. Scoop 12 balls ice cream mixture onto baking sheet. Freeze 1 hour.

3. Shape ice cream into balls, if necessary. Evenly sprinkle ice cream balls with salt. Insert sticks. Freeze 1 hour or until firm.

4. Melt chocolate in top of double boiler over simmering water, stirring occasionally.

5. Drizzle melted chocolate over pops. Freeze 30 minutes to 1 hour or until firm.

Makes 12 pops

·Cool Creations·

Salted Caramel Pops

S'more Pops

¼ cup plus 2 tablespoons fudge topping, divided
½ cup graham cracker crumbs
6 (3-ounce) paper or plastic cups or pop molds
1 cup marshmallow creme
¾ cup milk
1 cup vanilla ice cream
6 pop sticks

1. Place ¼ cup fudge topping in small microwavable bowl; microwave on HIGH 15 seconds. Stir until smooth.

2. Add graham cracker crumbs to melted fudge topping, mixing and mashing with fork until blended. Evenly divide mixture into cups; press mixture onto bottom of each cup, using wet fingers if necessary.

3. Combine marshmallow creme and remaining 2 tablespoons fudge topping in large microwavable bowl. Microwave on HIGH 20 to 30 seconds. Stir until smooth. Gradually whisk in milk.

4. Pour milk mixture in blender or food processor; add ice cream. Blend until smooth.

5. Pour mixture into cups over graham cracker base. Cover top of each cup with small piece of foil. Insert sticks through center of foil. Freeze 6 hours or until firm.

6. To serve, remove foil and peel away paper cups or gently twist frozen pops out of plastic cups.

Makes 6 pops

S'more Pops

Striped Peanut Butter & Jelly Pops

4 teaspoons grape jelly
Pop molds
1½ cups vanilla ice cream
¼ cup milk
2 tablespoons creamy peanut butter
1 cup coarsely chopped peanut butter sandwich cookies (about 2½ cups cookies)
Pop sticks

1. Place jelly in small microwavable bowl. Microwave on HIGH 20 seconds or until melted. Cool until mixture has consistency of thick syrup.

2. Using tip of small spoon, drip 1 teaspoon melted jelly inside rim of each mold to form stripes. Place molds in freezer until needed.*

3. Combine ice cream, milk and peanut butter in blender or food processor; blend until smooth. Add cookies; blend until smooth.

4. Pour peanut butter mixture into molds. Cover top of each mold with small piece of foil. Insert sticks through center of foil. Freeze 6 to 8 hours or until firm.

5. To remove pops from molds, remove foil and place bottoms of pops under warm running water until loosened. Press firmly on bottoms to release. (Do not twist or pull sticks.)

Makes 4 servings

Plastic pop molds must be used for this recipe. The jelly will not stick to paper or plastic cups.

Striped Peanut Butter & Jelly Pops

Chocolate-Hazelnut Pops

1 cup raw hazelnuts
⅓ cup chocolate-hazelnut spread*
1 pint (2 cups) vanilla ice cream
Pop sticks

Can be found in most supermarkets near the peanut butter.

1. Spread hazelnuts in single layer in heavy-bottomed skillet. Cook over medium heat 2 minutes, stirring frequently, or until skins begin to peel and nuts are lightly browned. Transfer to clean dish towel. Rub hazelnuts to remove skins. Cool completely. Chop and set aside.

2. Line two baking sheets with plastic wrap. Place plastic or acrylic cutting board in freezer 1 hour.

3. Meanwhile, drop 12 rounded teaspoonfuls chocolate-hazelnut spread onto one prepared baking sheet. Freeze 30 minutes or until firm.

4. Scoop ice cream onto frozen cutting board. Cut in chopped hazelnuts with pastry blender or two knives; fold and cut again. Repeat, working fast, until mixture is evenly incorporated.

5. Scoop 12 balls ice cream mixture onto second baking sheet. Place one frozen chocolate-hazelnut drop into center of each ball, gently pressing to enclose drop with ice cream.

6. Insert sticks. Freeze 2 hours or until firm.

Makes 12 pops

•Cool Creations•

Chocolate-Hazelnut Pops

Dreamy Orange Creamy Pops

  2 cups ice
1½ cups vanilla yogurt
¾ cup frozen orange juice concentrate
½ cup milk
¼ teaspoon vanilla
  Pop molds with lids

1. Combine ice, yogurt, orange juice concentrate, milk and vanilla in blender or food processor; blend until smooth.

2. Pour mixture into molds. Cover with lids. Freeze 6 hours or until firm.*

3. To remove pops from molds, place bottoms of pops under warm running water until loosened. Press firmly on bottoms to release. (Do not twist or pull lids.) *Makes 8 pops*

If using paper or plastic cups or molds without lids, cover each cup with small piece of foil. Freeze mixture 2 hours before inserting pop sticks through center of foil.

 *Tip* Frozen juice concentrate works great for frozen pops. Try any desired juice flavor and pair it with yogurt for a creamy fruity treat.

·Cool Creations·

Dreamy Orange Creamy Pops

Frozen Polar Bear Bites

1 medium banana
6 pop sticks
¼ cup creamy peanut butter
¼ cup mini marshmallows
2 tablespoons unsalted dry-roasted peanuts, chopped
1 tablespoon chocolate sprinkles

1. Cut banana into six equal pieces. Insert tips of sticks into peanut butter, then into banana pieces. Place on waxed paper-lined baking sheet.

2. Combine marshmallows, peanuts and chocolate sprinkles in shallow dish.

3. Place peanut butter in small microwavable bowl. Microwave on HIGH 20 to 30 seconds or until melted and smooth.

4. Dip each banana piece in melted peanut butter, turning to coat evenly. Roll in marshmallow mixture. Place on prepared baking sheet; let stand until set.

5. Freeze 6 to 8 hours or until firm.

Makes 6 servings

•Cool Creations•

Frozen Polar Bear Bites

Blackberry Swirl Pops

1¼ cups plain nonfat Greek yogurt
¼ cup milk
2 tablespoons sugar
2 tablespoons lime juice, divided
1 cup chopped blackberries
Pop molds
Pop sticks

1. Combine yogurt, milk, sugar and 1 tablespoon lime juice in blender or food processor; blend until smooth.

2. Combine blackberries and remaining 1 tablespoon lime juice in blender or food processor; blend until smooth.

3. Alternately layer yogurt mixture and blackberry mixture in molds.* Using thin knife, create swirls by drawing knife up and down through layers.

4. Cover top of each mold with small piece of foil. Insert sticks through center of foil. Freeze 4 hours or until firm.

5. To remove pops from molds, remove foil and place bottoms of pops under warm running water until loosened. Press firmly on bottoms to release. (Do not twist or pull sticks.)

Makes 6 pops

Plastic pop molds must be used for this recipe. The layers will not stay in place if using paper or plastic cups.

Tip: Another way to create thin swirls is by using a bamboo skewer or a thin round pop stick.

•Cool Creations•

Blackberry Swirl Pops

Almond Delight Pops

    4 ounces semisweet chocolate, divided
    1 cup chopped plain macaroons (about 10 to 12 macaroons)
1½ cups sliced almonds, toasted*
    1 pint (2 cups) vanilla frozen yogurt or ice cream
¼ cup strawberry jam
    Pop sticks

*To toast almonds, spread in single layer in heavy-bottomed skillet. Cook over medium heat 1 to 2 minutes, stirring frequently, until lightly browned. Remove from skillet immediately. Cool before using.

1. Place plastic or acrylic cutting board in freezer 1 hour. Line baking sheet with plastic wrap.

2. Meanwhile, melt 3 ounces chocolate in top of double boiler over simmering water, stirring occasionally. Remove from heat.

3. Gradually stir macaroon pieces into chocolate. Spread on prepared baking sheet. Freeze 30 minutes or until firm.

4. Spread almonds in shallow dish; set aside. Scoop frozen yogurt onto frozen cutting board. Cut in jam with pastry blender or two knives; fold and cut again. Gently mix in chocolate-covered macaroons.

5. Scoop 10 balls frozen yogurt mixture into almonds. Gently roll into balls, turning to coat and pressing almonds into frozen yogurt mixture. Place on prepared baking sheet. Freeze 1 hour.

6. Insert sticks. Freeze 1 to 2 hours or until firm.

7. Melt remaining 1 ounce chocolate in top of double boiler over simmering water, stirring occasionally.

8. Drizzle melted chocolate over pops. Freeze 30 minutes to 1 hour or until firm.

Makes 10 pops

•Cool Creations•

Almond Delight Pops

Party Time

Peachy Pops

1 package (16 ounces) frozen sliced peaches, softened, but not completely thawed
2 containers (6 ounces each) peach or vanilla yogurt
¼ cup honey
8 (5-ounce) paper or plastic cups or pop molds
8 pop sticks
   Assorted decorating sugars or sprinkles

1. Combine peaches, yogurt and honey in blender or food processor; blend until smooth.

2. Pour mixture into cups. Cover top of each cup with small piece of foil. Freeze 2 hours.

3. Insert sticks through center of foil. Freeze 6 hours or until firm.

4. Remove foil and peel away paper cups or gently twist frozen pops out of plastic cups.

5. Spread sugars on small plate; roll pops in sugar. Serve immediately or place in paper cups and return to freezer until ready to serve.   *Makes 8 pops*

Peachy Pops

Chocolate-Drizzled Grape Skewers

  2 cups seedless grapes (green, red or a combination of both)
    Bamboo skewers
¼ cup semisweet chocolate chips
¼ cup white chocolate chips

1. Wash grapes; remove stems. Dry completely with paper towel. Thread grapes on skewers. Place on waxed paper-lined baking sheet (see Tip).

2. Place semisweet chocolate chips in small microwavable bowl; microwave on HIGH 1 minute. Stir; microwave at 30-second intervals, stirring after each interval until smooth. Drizzle over grapes.

3. Place white chocolate chips in separate small microwavable bowl; microwave on HIGH 1 minute. Stir; microwave at 30-second intervals, stirring after each interval until smooth. Drizzle over grapes.

4. Freeze 2 hours before serving.

Makes 6 servings

Variation: You can also freeze the grapes completely and drizzle them with chocolate just before serving.

 Tip Use a rimmed baking sheet for this recipe. Rest the bamboo skewers against the rims and rotate them on the baking sheet to drizzle evenly with chocolate.

Chocolate-Drizzled Grape Skewers

Margarita Pops

 2 cup water
⅔ cup fresh lime juice (2 to 3 limes)
½ cup tequila
¼ cup sugar
 2 tablespoons Triple Sec or orange liqueur
 8 (2-ounce) plastic or paper cups or shot glasses
 8 pop sticks
   Coarse salt

1. Combine water, lime juice, tequila, sugar and Triple Sec in small saucepan; bring to a boil. Boil 1 minute or until sugar is dissolved, stirring constantly. Remove from heat. Cool to room temperature.

2. Pour mixture into cups. Cover top of each cup with small piece of foil. Freeze 2 hours.

3. Insert sticks through center of foil. Freeze 3 hours or until firm.

4. Remove foil and gently twist frozen pops out of plastic cups or peel away paper cups.*

5. Spread coarse salt on small plate. Roll pops in coarse salt. Serve immediately or place in plastic cups and return to freezer until ready to serve.   *Makes 8 pops*

If using shot glasses, place bottoms of glasses under cool running water until loosened. (Do not twist or pull sticks.) Or run a small thin knife around the inside edge of glasses to release pops.

Margarita Pops

Chocolate-Covered Espresso Pops

1 container (about 9 ounces) chocolate sprinkles
1 pint (2 cups) chocolate gelato or ice cream
1 cup chocolate-covered espresso beans, coarsely chopped*
   Pop sticks

Chocolate-covered espresso beans are available in fine supermarkets and gourmet food stores.

1. Line baking sheet with plastic wrap. Spread chocolate sprinkles in shallow dish; set aside.

2. Scoop gelato into chilled large metal bowl. Cut in chocolate-covered espresso beans with pastry blender or two knives; fold and cut again. Repeat, working fast, until mixture is evenly incorporated.

3. Scoop 24 rounded tablespoonfuls ice cream mixture onto sprinkles. Gently roll into balls, turning to coat and pressing mixture evenly into gelato. Place on prepared baking sheet. Freeze 1 hour.

4. Insert sticks. Freeze 1 hour or until firm.

Makes 24 pops

 Tip Use coffee stirrers for the pop sticks to add a pop of color and make these frozen treats more fun!

Chocolate-Covered Espresso Pops

Little Lemon-Basil Pops

1¼ cups plain nonfat Greek yogurt
¼ cup milk
　　Juice and grated peel of 1 lemon
2 tablespoons sugar
2 tablespoons chopped fresh basil
　　Ice cube trays
　　Pop sticks

1. Combine yogurt, milk, lemon juice, lemon peel, sugar and basil in blender or food processor; blend until smooth.

2. Pour mixture into ice cube trays. Freeze 2 hours.

3. Insert sticks. Freeze 4 to 6 hours or until firm.

4. To remove pops from trays, place bottoms of ice cube trays under warm running water until loosened. Press firmly on bottoms to release. (Do not twist or pull sticks.)

Makes 16 pops

Little Lemon-Basil Pops

White Sangria Pops

1 bottle dry, fruity white wine (such as Pinot Grigio)
1 cup white grape juice
1 cup seedless green grapes
1 orange, cut into ¼-inch slices
1 lemon, cut into ¼-inch slices
1 peach, peeled and cut into chunks
1 pear, peeled and cut into chunks
¼ cup sugar
   Pop molds
   Pop sticks

1. Heat wine in medium saucepan over low heat until reduced to about 2½ cups. Cool to room temperature, about 1 hour.

2. Combine reduced wine, grape juice, grapes, orange, lemon, peach, pear and sugar in large bowl or pitcher. Cover and refrigerate 8 hours or overnight.

3. Drain fruit; reserve liquid. Discard orange and lemon slices.

4. Evenly arrange remaining drained fruit in molds.* Evenly pour reserved liquid into molds. Cover top of each mold with small piece of foil. Insert sticks through center of foil. Freeze 8 hours or until firm.

5. To remove pops from molds, remove foil and place bottoms of pops under warm running water until loosened. Press firmly on bottoms to release. (Do not twist or pull sticks.)

Makes 8 servings

*Plastic pop molds must be used for this recipe. The fruit will not stay in place if using paper or plastic cups.

Serving Suggestion: Serve this party-pleasing treats in a pitcher or punch bowl.

White Sangria Pops

Chocolate-Covered Cheesecake Pops

1 package (8 ounces) cream cheese, at room temperature
⅓ cup sugar
1 teaspoon vanilla
1 cup whipping cream, chilled
¼ cup mini semisweet chocolate chips
Pop sticks
1 pound semisweet chocolate, chopped
Colored sprinkles

1. Beat cream cheese, sugar and vanilla in large bowl with electric mixer at medium-high speed until well blended.

2. Beat cream in separate large bowl at high speed until stiff peaks form. Gradually beat in cream cheese mixture, scraping down side of bowl after each addition. Gradually beat in chocolate chips. Cover and refrigerate 2 hours or until firm.

3. Line baking sheet with parchment paper. Gently roll cheesecake mixture into 24 balls. Place on baking sheet. Freeze 1 hour.

4. Insert sticks. Freeze 2 hours or until firm.

5. Melt chocolate in top of double boiler over simmering water, stirring occasionally.

6. Remove cheesecake balls from freezer. Dip in chocolate, rotating to coat evenly. Let excess chocolate drip off. Top evenly with sprinkles.

7. Return cheesecake pops to baking sheet. Freeze 1 hour or until firm.   *Makes 24 pops*

Chocolate-Covered Cheesecake Pops

Mojito Pops

¾ cup cold water
6 tablespoons light rum
2 tablespoons sugar
Juice of 1 lime
¼ cup fresh mint leaves
6 (2-ounce) paper or plastic cups or shot glasses
6 pop sticks

1. Combine water, rum, sugar and lime juice in small saucepan; bring to a simmer. Add mint, lightly mashing into mixture. Simmer 2 minutes. Remove from heat. Let stand 15 to 20 minutes to cool slightly.

2. Strain mixture into glass measuring cup; discard mint. Pour mixture into cups. Cover top of each cup with small piece of foil. Freeze 1 hour.

3. Insert sticks through center of foil. Freeze 2 hours or until firm.

4. To serve, remove foil and peel away paper cups or gently twist frozen pops out of plastic cups.*   *Makes 6 pops*

If using shot glasses, place bottoms of glasses under cool running water until loosened. (Do not twist or pull sticks.) Or run a small thin knife around the inside edge of glasses to release pops.

Mojito Pops

Mini Mexican Coffee Pops

¼ cup ground dark roast coffee
2 (3-inch) cinnamon sticks, broken into pieces
2 cups water
1½ teaspoons sugar
⅓ cup cinnamon-flavored half-and-half*
½ teaspoon vanilla
Ice cube trays
Picks or mini pop sticks

*You may use any flavor half-and-half or milk.

1. Place coffee and cinnamon sticks in filter basket of coffee maker. Add water to coffee maker and brew according to manufacturer's directions.

2. Remove coffee from heat. Stir in sugar until dissolved. Cool to room temperature, about 1 hour.

3. Add half-and-half and vanilla to cooled coffee. Pour mixture into ice cube trays. Freeze 2 hours.

4. Insert picks. Freeze 4 to 6 hours or until firm.

5. To remove pops from trays, place bottoms of ice cube trays under warm running water until loosened. Press firmly on bottoms to release. (Do not twist or pull picks.)

Makes about 32 pops

Mini Mexican Coffee Pops

Peanutty Pops

¾ cup chopped chocolate-covered peanut butter cups
1 pint (2 cups) vanilla ice cream
¼ cup crunchy peanut butter
2 cups chopped honey-roasted peanuts
Pop sticks

1. Freeze chocolate-covered peanut butter cups 20 to 30 minutes.*

2. Scoop ice cream into chilled large metal bowl. Cut in peanut butter cups and peanut butter with pastry blender or two knives; fold and cut again. Repeat, working quickly, until mixture is evenly incorporated. Cover and freeze 1 hour.

3. Line baking sheet with plastic wrap. Spread peanuts in shallow dish. Scoop 10 balls ice cream mixture into dish. Gently roll into balls, turning to coat and pressing peanuts evenly into ice cream mixture. Place on baking sheet. Freeze 1 hour.

4. Shape ice cream into balls, if necessary. Insert sticks. Freeze 1 hour or until firm.

Makes 10 pops

Freezing the peanut butter cups will make sure the chopped pieces remain as chunks and do not mix in with the ice cream.

 *Tip* To create the appearance of peanut butter ripples, line a baking sheet with parchment paper. Spread peanut butter into thin layer onto paper. Freeze 20 to 30 minutes. Peel paper away from peanut butter.

Peanutty Pops

Bellini Pops

1 ripe peach, peeled and chopped (about 1 cup)
4 teaspoons sugar
1 tablespoon orange liqueur
1½ teaspoons fresh lemon juice
½ cup dry white wine
6 (2-ounce) shot glasses or paper or plastic cups
6 pop sticks

1. Place peach in blender or food processor; blend until smooth.

2. Combine peach, sugar, orange liqueur and lemon juice in small bowl. Stir in wine.

3. Pour mixture into glasses. Cover top of each glass with small piece of foil. Freeze 2 hours.

4. Insert sticks through center of foil. Freeze 4 hours or until firm.

5. To remove pops from glasses, remove foil and place bottoms of glasses under warm running water until loosened. (Do not twist or pull sticks.) Or run a small thin knife around the inside edge of glasses to release pops. *Makes 6 pops*

Bellini Pops

Funky Flavors

Cheesecake Brownie Pops

1 package (about 21 ounces) brownie mix, plus ingredients to prepare mix
8 (5-ounce) paper or plastic cups or pop molds
1 pint (2 cups) vanilla frozen yogurt
2 cups whipped cream cheese
1 cup half-and-half
¼ cup sugar
¼ teaspoon vanilla
8 pop sticks

1. Prepare brownie in 13×9-inch baking pan according to package directions. Cool completely in pan on wire rack.

2. Using bottom of paper or plastic cups, cut eight circles out of brownies. Place circles in bottom of each cup.

3. Combine frozen yogurt, cream cheese, half-and-half, sugar and vanilla in blender or food processor; blend until smooth.

4. Pour mixture into cups over brownie base. Cover top of each cup with small piece of foil. Freeze 2 hours.

5. Insert sticks through center of foil. Freeze 4 hours or until firm.

6. To serve, remove foil and peel away paper cups or gently twist frozen pops out of plastic cups.
Makes 8 pops

Variation: If you want more brownies in this pop, stir ½ cup brownie chunks into the cheesecake mixture.

Cheesecake Brownie Pops

Berry Spice Pops

    1 cup mixed berries
½ cup sugar
    1 teaspoon grated lemon peel
½ teaspoon ground cinnamon
¼ teaspoon ground nutmeg
    1 cup vanilla frozen yogurt
    Pop molds with lids

1. Combine berries, sugar, lemon peel, cinnamon and nutmeg in small saucepan. Bring to a boil over medium heat. Mash hot berries with fork. Cook and stir 2 minutes. Cool to room temperature, about 1 hour.

2. Strain berries into medium bowl using fine-mesh sieve. Discard seeds.

3. Combine berry syrup and frozen yogurt in blender or food processor; blend until smooth.

4. Pour mixture into molds. Cover with lids. Freeze 8 hours or until firm.*

5. To remove pops from molds, place bottoms of pops under warm running water until loosened. Press firmly on bottoms to release. (Do not twist or pull lids.)   *Makes 4 pops*

If using paper or plastic cups or molds without lids, cover each cup with small piece of foil. Freeze mixture 2 hours before inserting pop sticks through center of foil.

 **Tip** You can use either fresh or frozen mixed berries in this recipe. The flavors work with any combination of berries.

•Funky Flavors•

Berry Spice Pops

Little Lemon-Pistachio Pops

  1 pint (2 cups) pistachio gelato
⅓ cup lemon curd
  2 tablespoons chopped jalapeño-flavored pistachio nuts*
    Grated peel of 1 lime
    Ice cube trays
    Pop sticks

You may substitute plain pistachio nuts.

1. Scoop gelato into chilled large metal bowl. Cut in lemon curd, pistachios and lime peel with pastry blender or two knives; fold and cut again. Repeat, working quickly, until mixture is evenly incorporated.

2. Evenly spoon mixture into ice cube trays. Freeze 30 minutes.

3. Insert sticks. Freeze 2 hours or until firm.

4. To remove pops from trays, place bottoms of ice cube trays under warm running water until loosened. Press firmly on bottoms to release. (Do not twist or pull sticks.)

Makes about 24 pops

Little Lemon-Pistachio Pops

Cinnamon-Honey Pops

1¼ cups plain nonfat Greek yogurt, divided
½ cup honey
¼ cup milk
1 tablespoon sugar
½ teaspoon ground cinnamon
½ teaspoon vanilla
    Pop molds or paper or plastic cups
    Pop sticks

1. Combine yogurt, honey, milk, sugar, cinnamon and vanilla in blender or food processor; blend until smooth.

2. Pour mixture into molds. Cover top of each mold with small piece of foil. Freeze 2 hours.*

3. Insert sticks through center of foil. Freeze 4 hours or until firm.

4. To remove pops from molds, remove foil and place bottoms of pops under warm running water until loosened. Press firmly on bottoms to release. (Do not twist or pull sticks.)

Makes 6 pops

If using pop molds with lids, skip step 3 and freeze until firm.

Cinnamon-Honey Pops

Avocado Lime Pops

1 avocado, peeled and pitted
1 cup sugar
  Juice and grated peel of 2 limes
1 cup milk
¼ teaspoon vanilla
6 (5-ounce) plastic or paper cups or pop molds
6 pop sticks

1. Combine avocado, sugar, lime juice, lime peel, milk and vanilla in blender or food processor; blend until smooth.

2. Pour mixture into cups. Cover top of each cup with small piece of foil. Freeze 1 hour.

3. Insert sticks through center of foil. Freeze 4 hours or until firm.

4. To serve, remove foil and gently twist frozen pops out of plastic cups or peel away paper cups.

Makes 6 pops

Avocado Lime Pops

Carrot Cake Pops

    4 jars (4 ounces each) baby food carrots
½ cup milk
    2 tablespoons granulated sugar
    2 tablespoons packed light brown sugar
    1 teaspoon ground cinnamon
½ teaspoon ground ginger
¼ teaspoon ground nutmeg
¼ teaspoon salt
    2 cups vanilla frozen yogurt
    Pop molds
½ cup chopped glazed walnuts
    Pop sticks

1. Combine carrots, milk, sugars, cinnamon, ginger, nutmeg and salt in blender or food processor; blend until smooth. Add frozen yogurt; blend until smooth.

2. Pour mixture into molds. Freeze 1 hour.

3. Stir mixture in molds until smooth and slushy. Stir 1 tablespoon walnuts into each mold. Smooth top of mixture with back of spoon. Cover top of each mold with small piece of foil. Freeze 1 hour.*

4. Insert sticks through center of foil. Freeze 4 hours or until firm.

5. To remove pops from molds, remove foil and place bottoms of pops under warm running water until loosened. Press firmly on bottoms to release. (Do not twist or pull sticks.)

Makes 8 pops

*If using pop molds with lids, skip step 4 and freeze until firm.

Carrot Cake Pops

Caramel Corn Pops

½ cup frozen corn, thawed
½ cup milk, plus additional if necessary
1 cup half-and-half
2 tablespoons granulated sugar
2 tablespoons packed light brown sugar
1 egg yolk
⅛ teaspoon vanilla
½ cup chopped glazed pecans
5 (3-ounce) paper or plastic cups or pop molds
5 pop sticks

1. Combine corn and ½ cup milk in large saucepan. Partially cover and cook over very low heat 30 minutes. (If milk evaporates completely, stir in additional ¼ cup.)

2. Stir half-and-half and sugars into corn mixture. Cook, uncovered, over low heat until sugar is dissolved and liquid comes to a simmer, stirring frequently.

3. Beat egg yolk in small bowl. Whisk about ¼ cup corn mixture into egg yolk. Add mixture to saucepan; cook over medium heat 10 minutes or until slightly thickened, stirring constantly. Remove from heat. Stir in vanilla. Let stand 30 minutes to cool slightly.

4. Cover and refrigerate mixture 2 hours or up to 1 day.

5. Place mixture in blender or food processor; blend until smooth. Cover and refrigerate 2 hours or until slightly thickened.

6. Stir in pecans. Pour mixture into cups. Cover top of each cup with small piece of foil. Freeze 1 hour.

7. Insert sticks through center of foil. Freeze 6 hours or until firm.

8. To serve, remove foil and peel away paper cups or gently twist frozen pops out of plastic cups.

Makes 5 pops

•Funky Flavors•

Caramel Corn Pops

Strawberry Lemonade Pops

½ can (12 ounces) frozen lemonade concentrate, partly thawed
 1 cup ice
½ cup sliced strawberries
½ cup water
 6 (3-ounce) paper or plastic cups or pop molds
 6 pop sticks

1. Combine lemonade concentrate, ice, strawberries and water in blender or food processor; blend until smooth.

2. Pour mixture into cups. Cover top of each cup with small piece of foil. Freeze 1 hour.

3. Insert sticks through center of foil. Freeze 4 hours or until firm.

4. To serve, remove foil and peel away paper cups or gently twist frozen pops out of plastic cups.

Makes 6 pops

Variation: If you love berries, make this pop even more flavorful and use raspberry lemonade concentrate.

 **Tip** These refreshing treats are perfect for a summertime barbecue.

Strawberry Lemonade Pops

Key Lime Pops

1¼ cups vanilla ice cream
⅔ cup frozen limeade concentrate
¼ cup milk
   Juice and grated peel of 1 lime
4 (5-ounce) paper or plastic cups or pop molds
4 pop sticks

1. Combine ice cream, limeade concentrate, milk, lime juice and lime peel in blender or food processor; blend until smooth.

2. Pour mixture into cups. Cover top of each cup with small piece of foil. Freeze 2 hours.

3. Insert sticks through center of foil. Freeze 6 hours or until firm.

4. To serve, remove foil and peel away paper cups or gently twist frozen pops out of plastic cups.

Makes 4 pops

 **Tip** To use cone-shaped paper cups, line a baking sheet with regular-shaped 5-ounce paper cups, bottom sides up. Cut a small hole in the bottom of each regular-shaped paper cup. Place a cone-shaped cup, tip side down, in the hole to hold the pop in place.

Key Lime Pops

Fluffy Peanut Butter Pops

1 cup crushed peanut butter sandwich cookies (about 2½ cups cookies), divided
½ cup plus 1 tablespoon milk, divided
4 (5-ounce) paper or plastic cups or pop molds
¾ cup marshmallow creme
¼ cup creamy peanut butter
1¼ cup vanilla ice cream
4 pop sticks

1. Combine ½ cup cookie crumbs and 1 tablespoon milk in small bowl, mixing and mashing with fork until blended. Press 2 tablespoons crumb mixture into each cup, using wet fingers if necessary.

2. Combine marshmallow creme and peanut butter in large microwavable bowl. Microwave on HIGH 20 to 30 seconds. Stir until smooth. Gradually whisk in remaining ½ cup milk.

3. Pour milk mixture in blender or food processor; add remaining ½ cup cookie crumbs and ice cream. Blend until smooth.

4. Pour mixture into cups over cookie base. Cover top of each cup with small piece of foil. Insert sticks through center of foil. Freeze 6 hours or until firm.

5. To serve, remove foil and peel away paper cups or gently twist frozen pops out of plastic cups.

Makes 4 pops

Fluffy Peanut Butter Pops

Holiday Delights

Valentine's Pops

½ cup (4 ounces) whipped cream cheese
2 cups cold milk, divided
1 package (4-serving size) white chocolate instant pudding and pie filling mix
½ cup thawed frozen raspberries, chopped
 Pop molds or paper or plastic cups
 Pop sticks

1. Stir cream cheese and ½ cup milk in large bowl until well blended. Add remaining 1½ cups milk and pudding mix; whisk 2 minutes. Cover and refrigerate 1 hour or until set.

2. Stir raspberries into mixture. Pour mixture into molds. Cover top of each mold with small piece of foil. Freeze 2 hours.*

3. Insert sticks through center of foil. Freeze 6 hours or until firm.

4. To remove pops from molds, remove foil and place bottoms of pops under warm running water until loosened. Press firmly on bottoms to release. (Do not twist or pull sticks.)

Makes 8 pops

If using pop molds with lids, skip step 3 and freeze until firm.

Valentine's Pops

St. Patty's Pops

½ cup crushed chocolate-covered mint cookies
⅓ cup plus 1 tablespoon milk, divided
3 (5-ounce) plastic or paper cups or pop molds
1¼ cups mint chocolate chip ice cream
3 pop sticks
6 tablespoons quick-hardening chocolate shell dessert topping

1. Combine cookie crumbs and 1 tablespoon milk in small bowl, mixing and mashing with fork until well blended. Press about 2 tablespoons crumb mixture into each cup, using wet fingers if necessary.

2. Combine remaining ⅓ cup milk and ice cream in blender or food processor; blend until smooth.

3. Pour mixture into cups over cookie base. Freeze 1 hour.

4. Insert sticks. Spoon 2 tablespoons chocolate shell topping into each cup over ice cream mixture. *Do not cover with foil.* Freeze 4 to 6 hours or until firm.

5. To serve, gently twist frozen pops out of plastic cups or peel away paper cups.

Makes 3 pops

St. Patty's Pops

Patriotic Pops

¾ cup plain nonfat Greek yogurt
2 tablespoons lemon juice, divided
1 tablespoon milk
1 cup sliced strawberries
½ cup blueberries
 Pop molds
 Pop sticks

1. Combine yogurt, 1 tablespoon lemon juice and milk in blender or food processor; blend until smooth.

2. Combine remaining 1 tablespoon lemon juice and strawberries in blender or food processor; blend until smooth.

3. Alternately layer blueberries, yogurt mixture and strawberry mixture into molds.* Cover top of each mold with small piece of foil. Insert sticks through center of foil. Freeze 4 hours or until firm.

4. To remove pops from molds, remove foil and place bottoms of pops under warm running water until loosened. Press firmly on bottoms to release. (Do not twist or pull sticks.)

Makes 4 pops

Plastic pop molds must be used for this recipe. The fruit will not stay in place if using paper or plastic cups.

 *Tip* Greek yogurt is yogurt from which much of the liquid or "whey" has been drained before use. It is available in most major grocery stores.

·Holiday Delights·

Patriotic Pops

Bleeding Pops

1 cup vanilla frozen yogurt
6 (5-ounce) paper or plastic cups or pop molds
1 cup raspberry sorbet
6 pop sticks
Red decorating gel

1. Place frozen yogurt in small microwavable bowl; microwave on LOW (30%) 10 seconds. Whisk and microwave at 10-second intervals until frozen yogurt reaches pourable consistency (about 5 times).

2. Evenly pour frozen yogurt into cups. Freeze 1 hour or until just set.

3. Place sorbet in small microwavable bowl; microwave on LOW (30%) 10 seconds. Whisk and microwave at 10-second intervals until sorbet reaches pourable consistency (about 5 times).

4. Evenly pour sorbet over frozen yogurt layer. Cover top of each cup with small piece of foil. Freeze 30 minutes.

5. Insert sticks through center of foil. Freeze 5 hours or until firm.

6. Remove foil and peel away paper cups or gently twist frozen pops out of plastic cups.

7. Pipe decorating gel down pops, allowing gel to drip down sides. Serve immediately.

Makes 6 pops

Bleeding Pops

Pumpkin Pie Pops

½ cup canned pumpkin pie mix
½ cup milk
¼ teaspoon vanilla
1½ cups vanilla ice cream
6 (5-ounce) paper or plastic cups or pop molds
2 containers (4 ounces each) prepared refrigerated vanilla pudding, divided
3 teaspoons brown sugar, divided
6 cinnamon sticks or pop sticks

1. Combine pumpkin pie mix, milk and vanilla in blender or food processor; blend until smooth. Add ice cream; blend until smooth.

2. Pour 2 tablespoons mixture into each cup. Freeze 30 to 45 minutes or until just set. Cover and refrigerate remaining pumpkin mixture.

3. Combine 1 container vanilla pudding and 1½ teaspoons brown sugar; mix well. Spoon 1 tablespoon mixture over pumpkin mixture in each cup. Freeze 30 to 45 minutes or until just set.

4. Pour 2 tablespoons pumpkin mixture over pudding mixture in each cup. Freeze 30 to 45 minutes or until just set. Cover and refrigerate remaining pumpkin mixture.

5. Combine remaining 1 container pudding and 1½ teaspoons brown sugar; mix well. Spoon 1 tablespoon mixture over pumpkin mixture in each cup. Freeze 30 to 45 minutes or until just set.

6. Pour 1 tablespoon pumpkin mixture over pudding mixture in each cup. Cover top of each cup with small piece of foil. Freeze 30 to 45 minutes or until just set.

7. Gently insert cinnamon sticks through center of foil. Freeze 6 hours or until firm.

8. To serve, remove foil and peel away paper cups or gently twist frozen pops out of plastic cups.

Makes 6 pops

Pumpkin Pie Pops

Apple Pie Pops

1 refrigerated pie crust (½ of 15-ounce package)
1½ teaspoons packed brown sugar
1 tablespoon milk
4 (5-ounce) paper or plastic cups or pop molds
1¼ cups vanilla ice cream
1 cup apple pie filling
1 teaspoon pumpkin pie spice
4 pop sticks

1. Preheat oven to 450°F. Line baking sheet with parchment paper. Let pie crust stand at room temperature 15 minutes.

2. Roll pie crust onto prepared baking sheet. Prick with fork. Bake 10 to 12 minutes or until golden brown. Cool completely on baking sheet.

3. Crumble pie crust. Combine ½ cup crumbs and brown sugar in small bowl; mix well. Discard remaining crumbs or save for future use. Add milk to crumb mixture, mixing and mashing with fork until well blended. Press about 2 tablespoons crumb mixture into each cup, using wet fingers if necessary.

4. Combine ice cream, pie filling and pumpkin pie spice in blender or food processor; blend until smooth.

5. Pour ice cream mixture into cups over crumb base. Cover top of each cup with small piece of foil. Insert sticks through center of foil. Freeze 6 hours or until firm.

6. To serve, remove foil and peel away paper cups or gently twist frozen pops out of plastic cups.

Makes 4 pops

Holiday Delights

Apple Pie Pops

Gingery Cheesecake Pops

1 package (8 ounces) cream cheese, at room temperature
⅓ cup plus 2 teaspoons sugar, divided
¼ cup minced crystallized ginger (optional)
1 teaspoon vanilla
1 cup whipping cream
¾ cup gingersnap cookie crumbs (about 15 to 18 cookies)
¼ cup ground pecans*
¼ teaspoon ground cinnamon
Pop sticks

To grind pecans, place in blender or food processor; blend until thoroughly ground with a dry, not pasty, texture.

1. Beat cream cheese, ⅓ cup sugar, crystallized ginger, if desired, and vanilla in large bowl with electric mixer at medium-high speed until well blended.

2. Beat cream in separate large bowl at high speed until stiff peaks form. Gradually beat in cream cheese mixture, scraping down side of bowl after each addition. Cover and refrigerate 2 hours or until firm.

3. Line baking sheet with plastic wrap. Combine gingersnap crumbs, ground pecans, remaining 2 teaspoons sugar and cinnamon in shallow dish.

4. Scoop 24 rounded tablespoonfuls cheesecake mixture into gingersnap mixture. Gently roll into balls, turning to coat and pressing mixture evenly into cheesecake. Place on prepared baking sheet. Freeze 1 hour.

5. Insert sticks. Freeze 2 hours or until firm.   *Makes 24 pops*

Serving Suggestion: For your holiday party, serve these pops in decorative miniature foil or paper baking cups. To make them even fancier, tie a ribbon around each stick.

Gingery Cheesecake Pops

Merry Mint Pops

1 pint (2 cups) peppermint ice cream
½ cup crushed peppermint candies (about 12 round candies)
½ cup chocolate sprinkles
   Pop sticks

1. Line baking sheet with plastic wrap. Scoop 14 rounded tablespoonfuls ice cream onto baking sheet. Freeze 2 hours or until firm.

2. Combine crushed peppermints and sprinkles in shallow dish. Gently roll ice cream into balls in mixture, turning to coat and pressing mixture evenly into ice cream. Return to baking sheet.*

3. Insert sticks. Freeze 2 hours or until firm.   *Makes 14 pops*

If ice cream melts on baking sheet, place baking sheet and ice cream in freezer 30 minutes before continuing. If ice cream is too hard, let stand 1 to 2 minutes before rolling in mixture.

 *Tip* This recipe is best served the same day it is made. The candies will become soft and sticky over time.

•Holiday Delights•

Merry Mint Pops

Winter Wonderland Pops

  1 pint (2 cups) vanilla ice cream
  ½ cup coarsely chopped macadamia nuts
  ½ cup chopped dried pineapple
  2 tablespoons minced crystallized ginger
  2 cups shredded, sweetened coconut, toasted*
    Pop sticks

To toast coconut, spread in single layer in heavy skillet. Cook over medium heat 1 to 2 minutes until lightly browned, stirring frequently. Remove from skillet immediately. Cool before using.

1. Scoop ice cream into chilled large metal bowl. Cut in macadamia nuts, pineapple and ginger with pastry blender or two knives; fold and cut again. Repeat, working quickly, until mixture is evenly incorporated. Cover and freeze 1 hour.

2. Line baking sheet with plastic wrap. Spread coconut in shallow dish. Scoop 10 scant ¼ cupfuls ice cream mixture into coconut. Gently roll ice cream into balls, turning to coat and pressing coconut evenly into ice cream. Place on baking sheet. Freeze 1 hour.

3. Insert sticks. Freeze 1 hour or until firm.

Makes 10 pops

 **Tip** Crystallized ginger can be found in the spice aisle of the grocery store.

Winter Wonderland Pops

·Index·

•Index•

Metric Conversion Chart

VOLUME MEASUREMENTS (dry)

$^1/_8$ teaspoon = 0.5 mL
$^1/_4$ teaspoon = 1 mL
$^1/_2$ teaspoon = 2 mL
$^3/_4$ teaspoon = 4 mL
1 teaspoon = 5 mL
1 tablespoon = 15 mL
2 tablespoons = 30 mL
$^1/_4$ cup = 60 mL
$^1/_3$ cup = 75 mL
$^1/_2$ cup = 125 mL
$^2/_3$ cup = 150 mL
$^3/_4$ cup = 175 mL
1 cup = 250 mL
2 cups = 1 pint = 500 mL
3 cups = 750 mL
4 cups = 1 quart = 1 L

VOLUME MEASUREMENTS (fluid)

1 fluid ounce (2 tablespoons) = 30 mL
4 fluid ounces ($^1/_2$ cup) = 125 mL
8 fluid ounces (1 cup) = 250 mL
12 fluid ounces (1$^1/_2$ cups) = 375 mL
16 fluid ounces (2 cups) = 500 mL

WEIGHTS (mass)

$^1/_2$ ounce = 15 g
1 ounce = 30 g
3 ounces = 90 g
4 ounces = 120 g
8 ounces = 225 g
10 ounces = 285 g
12 ounces = 360 g
16 ounces = 1 pound = 450 g

DIMENSIONS

$^1/_{16}$ inch = 2 mm
$^1/_8$ inch = 3 mm
$^1/_4$ inch = 6 mm
$^1/_2$ inch = 1.5 cm
$^3/_4$ inch = 2 cm
1 inch = 2.5 cm

OVEN TEMPERATURES

250°F = 120°C
275°F = 140°C
300°F = 150°C
325°F = 160°C
350°F = 180°C
375°F = 190°C
400°F = 200°C
425°F = 220°C
450°F = 230°C

BAKING PAN SIZES

Utensil	Size in Inches/Quarts	Metric Volume	Size in Centimeters
Baking or Cake Pan (square or rectangular)	8 × 8 × 2	2 L	20 × 20 × 5
	9 × 9 × 2	2.5 L	23 × 23 × 5
	12 × 8 × 2	3 L	30 × 20 × 5
	13 × 9 × 2	3.5 L	33 × 23 × 5
Loaf Pan	8 × 4 × 3	1.5 L	20 × 10 × 7
	9 × 5 × 3	2 L	23 × 13 × 7
Round Layer Cake Pan	8 × 1½	1.2 L	20 × 4
	9 × 1½	1.5 L	23 × 4
Pie Plate	8 × 1¼	750 mL	20 × 3
	9 × 1¼	1 L	23 × 3
Baking Dish or Casserole	1 quart	1 L	—
	1½ quart	1.5 L	—
	2 quart	2 L	—